# SURVIVING COVID-19:
# A GUIDE FOR SMALL BUSINESSES
### (and then some)

By: Scott Annes

Published by Businessaire, Inc.
Copyright © 2020 Scott Annes
All rights reserved.

## Introduction

It is time to exhale. Moreover, it is time to go outside and take a breath without some cloth covering over half of your face that makes your phone's face recognition software unable to verify that you are you. While wearing my mask the other day Siri told me that it was not Halloween and that she did not find any masquerade parties on my calendar. She then looked at my bank app and told me that I was "okay" for the time being and that I likely did not have the agility and poise to become a bank robber anyway. She then scanned the internet and saw more pictures of people wearing masks as she commented that she does not understand the new fashion trend but that in her opinion it did not work for me. She also commented that I have missed at least two haircuts that had been on my schedule. Oh that Siri. She is a peach!

Just the same, my conversation with Siri told me a lot about where things stand in

COVID land. As that pain in the ass microscopic virus gets ready to sail out of port like the *USS Comfort,* I realized that we need to look at things from a different perspective. (By the way, why do we have a ship called the *USS Comfort?* Do we have a *USS Relax?* How about a *USS Kick-back?* Oh that's right, if we had a *USS Kick-back* people would think that you were talking about the *USS Chicago.*).

In questioning (perhaps even interrogating) me the way she did, Siri had provided some much needed perspective for me. She did not understand Coronavirus. Why should she? Just like many of the people with no first hand experience with it, if it does not affect her personally then why should she care? Yet, more than that, her questions gave me pause to consider what has happened since the last time when things were normal. Do you recall when that was? Think about it. It will come to you. Did you say Superbowl weekend? Then you are correct.

It was roughly in early February that things were not quite so "different" as they have been since then. ("Different" is my euphemism of the day - nice, right?). So, since February things have not been the same. Who am I kidding? The word is not "different" the word is "shitty." Since roughly February of 2020, things have been shitty! Since that time we have had the virus, the unplugging of the economy, the shut downs, the face masks, social distancing, hundreds of thousands of infections worldwide and tens of thousands of deaths in the US depending upon who is counting and their idea of arithmetic.

So, in retrospect, I apologize for saying that things were "different" when indeed they really have been shitty.

Meanwhile, depending on where you live in the country, you may either know someone who has it, or worse, you may know someone who has succumbed to it. Whereas, in other parts of the country, you may not have any direct experience with the people most affected. The good thing for you folks who have not encountered it first hand is that our leaders, the media, advertisers and just about everyone have made sure that the suffering caused by the virus has been shared to the maximum extent possible. Indeed, COVID-19 is an equal opportunity disaster and everyone seems to be entitled to a misery stimulus payment from it.

For all that we know, some people seem to be immune to the disease but no one will be spared its effect. The people with the most influence have made sure of that. We are told that the disease affects everybody. We are all told that we have an obligation to feel bad. We are advised that we need to be perpetually somber as we think about what it is doing to so many. If you are not actually infected then it is implied that you should feel guilty about that fact. It is as if people feel that if you do not actually suffer from the disease then the least you can do is feel perpetually despondent. Nothing is to be enjoyed in its wake. There will be no sports and no fun. You cannot go to a bar or to the movies or to a playground. You cannot take your frustrations out in the gym. You are relegated to your home as if the government grounded you or sent you to your room without telling you why you are being punished. You cannot go to the beach or attend a religious service. You are left in a state of perpetual contentious curfew. Everything has been redesigned so as to make you feel terrible.

    Here is a question. *Should* we feel constant despair about the COVID-19 outbreak? Well, as you look at it, the virus is ravaging the elderly. I am aware that these are the same people who many did not visit regularly before the pandemic but we do care about them nonetheless. These are the same people who tried to call you during the Superbowl and but-for caller ID you might have taken their call but instead you called them back on Monday when you were taking the day off to be hung over.

    In addition to what it is doing to our seniors, the virus is making other people very sick. We should feel bad about that. Of course, we have no evidence that it is any more pervasive than the flu in how severely it affects most people. Like many, I had the flu in January but I do not seem to recall people shutting down businesses and posting social media campaigns about how everyone was in it with me.

If asking whether we *should* feel bad about COVID-19 sounds cold and heartless then fear not. I will likely be appropriately bashed on social media for having even raised the question. I will be taken out of context for having the uninhibited gall to try to help people gain perspective in all of this. I will be scapegoated for no other reason than that I am an "enemy" that you can see. People will forget that I am merely commenting on the enemy that we cannot see without the assistance of a microscope.

Coronavirus is an example of when microorganisms behave badly. It has been a terrible house guest to many of the humans who have hosted it. It has been such a pain in the ass that it has wreaked havoc on an entire species who have had to react and, in many cases, overreact to it. It caught us unprepared much the like 9/11 terrorists and it has exacted a heavy price on us physically, emotionally and . . . . dare I say it . . . financially?

If you are reading this then perhaps that

last word caught your eye. If you are in business then perhaps you have considered how the pandemic has affected you *financially*. There is nothing wrong in that. It has profoundly affected the world economies and has undoubtedly ruined people. It has rendered itself a tragedy of epic proportions. It has killed many and in its wake it has left many who will never have contracted it to die a slow and tortured death of heartache and poverty.

So, when I say what I have about this particular coronavirus and its effect, I am not being insensitive to those who have contracted it or who have become sick or died. I grieve for them as we all do and rightly should. However, in its wake, the disease has killed off many small and some large businesses. These were people's livelihoods and in many cases their dreams and now many of them shall perish.

I feel terrible for those people. They did absolutely nothing wrong and yet the virus and our reaction to it has virtually wiped them out. They took the prescribed precautions and they tried to help others and still they lost their businesses. Based on what anybody knew at the time, none of these folks were irresponsible and yet they still have had to pay a price as if they were. Businesspeople affected by the virus have gotten screwed and that is more than merely a shame, it is a tragedy!

For their troubles, if they dare ask when they might be able to reopen and get back to normal then they are vilified by the overtly conscientious "thought police" and "mask-shamers." In some instances, all they are seeking is some level of hope and in response they are castigated for being insensitive. They are told to shut up and just keep sacrificing. In their defense, one could argue that it was not that the virus killed them but rather that it did not kill them quickly enough.

As for me, I will not apologize for being sympathetic to these folks. Lives have been lost in the wake of the pandemic but for many in business large and small, their lives have been ruined. Many have philosophically suggested in the past that if a nuclear bomb goes off then those who died immediately are the lucky ones and the rest who have to try to survive in the aftermath suffer the most. Without disrespecting the lives lost to COVID - 19, I find the shattered dreams and livelihoods of those left in its wake no less a tragedy. Picking up the pieces when this is all over will be hard enough without seeing how it has emptied our bank accounts and destroyed the very means by which we feed ourselves.

Feeling as bad as I do for the businesses affected and lost in the wake of the pandemic, I wrote this book to give some people perspective and, perhaps even more important, to give them some hope. I have provided a dozen strategies that I feel might be useful in navigating the new waters in which we have splashed down. I chose a dozen but there are certainly more. You can get those strategies and ideas from good businesspeople who have dealt with tragedies. You should listen to those folks. There is a lot to be learned from those who have suffered and survived.

If my introduction to this point seems dark well then I have set the tone properly. Things are somewhat bleak right now and I am not about to put fresh paint on cracked plaster. At this point, we have to fix the plaster. We may even need to make it so it is not likely to get broken so easily ever again. It will take work, determination and ingenuity. Those characteristics are entrepreneurs' stock and trade however and so they should take solace in the fact that they are already equipped with what they need.

Perhaps when this book is done we will have added one more asset to our entrepreneurs' tool box: hope. The truth of the matter is that we are likely to actually come through this thing. We will continue to suffer some battle scars but we might just make it to the other side. This book is intended to provide some reasons to maintain that hope. That hope may prove an important element in creating a vision of a time when this crisis has passed. If you can convince a rational and logical person that there is a reason to hope then you really can change the world.

So to our entrepreneurs, this book is

faithfully and unapologetically dedicated to you. Make of it what you will. I am eternally indebted to you for the inspiration you give me in my quest to help small businesses. If this book can provide some level of hope, or humor or perspective or even some respite from the crisis, then I will have achieved my purpose. I do this for businesspeople. God bless you all!

## Chapter 1
## Strategy # 1: Separate Myths from Reality

*I have a tough time empathizing with hypochondriacs, I just can't seem to imagine what they seem to imagine is making them feel ill.*

Businesspeople, by nature, are risk-takers. They obtain information and then analyze it so as to make decisions. The best information that they can use is derived from concrete facts. However, facts are not always easy to ascertain and so they are left to rely upon assumptions. Is it critical that they use assumptions which are based on *facts* in order to make decisions? These assumptions usually incorporate intuition, gut feeling, statistical analysis, things businesspeople have learned from experience and a whole host of other elements so as to help them make decisions. Businesspeople must be critical of the assumptions that they are relying upon and that is where our discussion brings us back to our premise that by necessity, our assumptions need to be based on *facts*. If businesspeople rely upon a fact and that *fact* ultimately proves to be wrong then they will likely make a wrong decision.

The consequences of wrong decisions can be devastating in such instances. Just think about all the times that you relied upon an incorrect assumption of facts to make a decision and then learned that the assumption was wrong. The result was probably not what you wanted and certainly not what you anticipated.

So, when it comes to the COVID-19 crisis, businesspeople have to assess facts in order to form assumptions from which to make decisions. Finding these facts has been the tricky part however because so many people have spoken with so much authority as to have us believe that they are providing *facts* when the truth is that they are actually providing guesses at best. For all that we know, some of these guesses may be right. So far, many of their guesses have proven not to be correct however and that is one of the major problems that we are having in managing the crisis and responding to it.

As one thinks about it, therein lies the biggest obstacle in handling this mess. So far, we cannot trust the information being provided to us from the so-called experts. We have lots of people with all sorts of political and personal agendas telling us what we need to do in order to save lives and stop the spread of the disease. We have people submitting opinions and stating them as if they were facts. We have people providing statistics and models that supposedly provide the basis of these learned opinions and then what actually happens never seems to match whatever data they allegedly relied upon in reaching their conclusions.

Perhaps the most ironic thing about all of this is that the people expressing opinions and purporting to be authorities preface every pronouncement by telling everyone that this is unprecedented and that we have never had to deal with anything like this before. So, what they are saying is that they have no actual experience with this problem and so they will not guarantee what will happen but we should take their advice anyway. It is sort of like a podiatrist telling you "well, I've never done an appendectomy but I have been studying models and statistics on it so I think we can give it a shot. Nurse, hand me a scalpel please."

So here we are. We have experts who do not know anything really. We have politicians who, though somewhat clueless, feel that they can save lives with an abundance of caution while killing businesses without so much as a second thought. We have a media that feels that they can report any fiction that they like for the sake of their own agenda and pedal it as news and we have social media that blows up with rumor after rumor of impending doom.

We have all of this anxiety, confusion, and ignorance and you have a business to run (or not)! You need information to make decisions for your business and it seems none of that information is coming from *facts*. There is no shortage of opinions, theories, statistics and guesses all of which are used to form the only assumptions available for you to incorporate into your decision-making. In the absence of facts, all you can do is to form assumptions relying upon the information - regardless of how uncertain it is - as to what you should do. It tends to make you realize how much we take certainty for granted.

Adding to all of this uncertainty is the fact that many of the opinions and much of the conjecture that we are getting are coming from people who lack objectivity. There are people who provide opinions based on their own subjective conclusions and then they develop a contrived narrative to support the opinion. The media elevates certain people to "expert" status for supporting their agenda while overlooking others who are more qualified but might espouse opinions contrary to their agenda. Essentially, we are left with assumptions based on opinions that are being presented by experts who are not being objective. Their personal feelings may be clouding their judgment to reach conclusions of which they were predisposed. It is as if they knew what they wanted the answer to be and then decided to manipulate the numbers on the other side of the equation to reach that answer. Assumptions reached under these circumstances are hardly useful and may undermine your decision-making.

In the bigger picture, what this says about our world is even more disturbing. The thing that has exacerbated the COVID -19 crisis is our current cultural environment. Our political, economic, generational and philosophical divisions have contributed to not being able to properly put this mess into perspective. We cannot even agree on how serious the crisis is. There are some people hunkered down in their hermitically sealed basements with masks worrying themselves to death while others are out and about as if there is no threat at all. In this instance, neither can genuinely appreciate the perspective of the other while the former thinks that the latter has a death wish and the latter thinks the former is overly dramatic.

Without at least some degree of perspective then we have only limited our likelihood of overcoming this. Sadly, there are people who are invested in us not coming through this successfully which is also indicative of how divided we are.

As business owners, we have to make a conscious decision not to rely upon what people are saying about the crisis and focus on what we actually know.  Here is what we know for sure: COVID - 19 is a disease that affects humans and some of the people who get it will die.

Here is everything else that we know for certain about COVID-19: . . . . . . . . . . . . . . . . . .
. . . . . . . . . . .

That is not a typo.  We really do not seem to know much more than that it affects humans and that some people who contract it will die. We have no idea what percentage will die from it but thus far it has been a relatively small percentage.  We have no idea how many humans actually have contracted the virus.

We suspect that it causes some people to exhibit symptoms and become ill but that others show few or no symptoms.  We suspect that if affects the elderly and other people who are more vulnerable because of various health-related issues.  We suspect that it is highly contagious. Many of these things have proven more or less anecdotally to be true but given how little else we know about this particular coronavirus, many of these facts can be challenged one way or another.

Meanwhile, we know even less about all the prescriptions and efforts that we are taking to stop the virus. Maybe masks work or maybe they do not. In some cases we have found that they do not. We do not know if social distancing really stops the spread. Despite all of our extreme efforts to social distance, people are still getting the disease, We do not know if stay-at-home orders work or not. We do seem to know that stay-at-home orders are killing off businesses. That seems fairly well established.

We do not know what cures the virus. Some medical professionals have insisted that hydroxychloroquine works. There is anecdotal evidence to support this but some medical professionals say no. It seems odd that we have to listen to the medical professionals who insist on imposing the stay-at-home orders but not the ones who are in favor of potential medicine that might help the afflicted.

Oh, by the way, excuse me but I forgot one other thing that we do know for sure. It has been largely ignored by the press and on social media and by just about everyone invested in the panic that the pandemic is raising yet it is no small fact. We also know that some people (dare I say a profoundly significant percentage) recover from it.

The bad news for you as you attempt to run your business in the wake of this mess is that we do not have a lot of reliable information to go on. Therefore, we need to be very careful when it comes to our assumptions based on the information we have. We must consider the source and whether we are getting our information from someone with an agenda. Then, we have to make decisions based on what we know for a fact and not based on what we merely suspect. If you do not have facts then make an educated guess but do not invest heavily into guessing.

So perhaps the only thing you can do as you analyze the information necessary to navigate your business through COVID-19 is to avoid fooling yourself. As you separate the myths from reality and steady the ship in order to move forward, you would be wise to let go of your own agendas and your predispositions and look at this thing for what it is. It is a mess. Do not wallow in it and do not become overwhelmed by it. It is a mess.

The good news for you that in business, we deal with messes every day and there is no reason to think that you will not handle this one. It might be bigger than some of the messes that you have seen in the past but do not let that discourage you. To the extent that the mess affects your business then clean that part of it up and keep moving forward.

Based on this rationale, in the end, here is what we know. The "crisis" is really just a "mess." Being in business is really just a series of cleaning up messes. Messes come with the territory. Cleaning them up is what you do. This is a pretty big mess and cleaning it up seems daunting. But, what choice do you have? If you quit then you still have the mess. If you try to clean it up then you might just survive and once again be successful and prosperous. It does not seem like a choice to me but then again, what do I know? I am just a guy who cleans up messes.

## Chapter 2
## Strategy # 2: Avoid Getting It

*When a guy steps up at an AA meeting and says, "hi, my name is Scott and it's been . . . ." and then before he says anything else, he looks at his watch to determine when he last had a drink, then it is a safe bet that he still has a problem.*

Remember the 1976 made-for-TV movie *The Boy in the Plastic Bubble?* It is okay if you do not, most people probably do not recall it. It was the story of a young man, played by a very young John Travolta, who was required to spend his entire life inside a hermetically sealed plastic bubble that prevented him from being infected with any air-born or other type of pathogens. As one thinks about it, there might be some inspiration there. Maybe all that we need for

America to survive COVID-19 is 327,000,000 of those plastic bubbles. Then we can return to work and our daily lives with just that single modification. It will seem a little inconvenient at first and most likely will usher in the distinction of our species as it would render procreation impossible but . . . . it will keep us safe.

Without the hyperbole of plastic bubbling the population, the point for all of us is to avoid spreading the virus. There is a school of thought about "herd immunity" and I guess my feeling would be that there is some logic to that. Nonetheless, if you can avoid contracting or spreading the disease by taking *reasonable* steps then I would say do it.

Notice that I said *reasonable* steps. In attempting to preserve our health and safety, the debate has become one of what is *reasonable?* Some steps are more or less innocuous such as wearing masks. Some steps, such as locking ourselves in our homes as if they are nuclear fallout shelters, not so much. The concept of *reasonable* is subjective and that is why we are having the debate. Reasonable people could disagree as to what our response to COVID -19 should be.

One of the many problems that we have with COVID-19 is that it has hit at a precisely opportune time in history. We have a world full of people who exhibit a great deal of fear and worry. There are those who are so dedicated to safety concerns that they will forego everything else just to be safe. They have spawned a generation that is more fearful than most of just about everything. These people have even created "safe zones" and "safe spaces" that protect them from being assailed by so much as a contrary point of view. As a result, many today are more prone to overreaction to a perceived threat than at any other time in recent history.

Things have been pretty good for most people for the last few years and they are finding that they have more to lose than ever before. This naturally makes people protective of the things and the lifestyle they enjoy and so they tend to overcompensate when it comes to preserving what they have. Some will undoubtedly take things to the extreme in these instances. Ironically, that is where the real danger lurks.

Into this world along comes a virus that easily takes up residence in human hosts and can travel among us fairly easily. It infiltrates us through our interactions and spreads. Once we are aware of it, we react. We become aware that the virus can cause death and our sense of self preservation takes over. We agree to forego our liberty and we shelter-in-place in order to prevent further spread of the virus and, perhaps somewhat selfishly, we seek to prevent becoming infected ourselves.

It seems ironic that in a society where humans regularly indulge in smoking and illicit drug use and alcohol abuse and reckless driving and a whole myriad of activities that could kill us, we overreact to a virus that actually kills a small percentage of those who are afflicted. Just the same, in our world today the virus has become the world's most prolific boogeyman. The various forms of media have fanned the flame that has ignited the fear in us and so we are left with no choice but to overreact to the threat caused by the virus.

Think about it. In reacting to COVID-19 we have completely pulled the plug on the economy perhaps causing irreparable harm to it. I have a difficult time reconciling this as I think about the effect this has had on small and moderate sized businesses. I often wonder if years from now we will look back and wonder what we were thinking by turning off the economy as if that were a *reasonable* option.

Nonetheless, although I would have thought that turning off the economy was impossible, we did it. Politicians who lack the capacity to empathize with business and who may not have adequately thought through the consequences of shutting down the entire system, took the initiative and pulled the plug. They closed us. They allowed some businesses to remain as "essential" but otherwise they imposed the ultimate restriction and penultimate regulation that precedes closing businesses permanently.

And in the wake of the actions by these

politicians pedaling pandemic panic, businesses yearned to survive. They adapted at a rate of speed that seems miraculous by most standards. It is a testament to the creativity and determination of our businesspeople that we have found ways to do business in the wake of unyieldingly excessive regulation and restriction. It is beyond a shame that they have been so fiercely subjugated by politicians who insist that they are doing this "for our own good." If they really want to do anything for "our own good" then allow business to resume with minimal restrictions that make sense and suspend all taxes for a period equal to the amount of time that we were shut down.

And, when our political leaders say that they cannot suspend taxes for that period then would someone from the press please ask the question: "why not?" And then when they answer that "the government needs its tax money to operate" then please follow up with the question: "so are you suggesting that businesses did not need money during the time that they were mandatorily closed by your orders?"

But I digress. My resentment for the autocrats that assume public office and wield power that they do not actually possess with impunity notwithstanding, what has happened has happened. It is spilled milk that remains rotting on the floor and stinking to high heaven. We are where we are and that is that. The initial reaction to COVID-19 cannot be undone. All that any of us in business can do now is to overcome it.

So, perhaps the first thing you can do for your purposes as a business owner is to take steps not to contract the virus. Moreover, take steps not to have your staff get the virus and by all reasonable means take steps to avoid having your customers get the virus while interacting with your business.

Once again, the important word here is *reasonable*. What is *reasonable* in this situation? Well, wearing masks may seem silly but in the grand scheme of things, it is no big deal so why not wear the masks? However, my dear wife, a nurse and otherwise one of the most brilliant people I know whose only lack of judgment came in agreeing to marry me, insists that most people do not wear the masks correctly. They need to be over the nose and over your mouth and fit in such a way as to prevent air from freely escaping without passing through at least some part of the mask. That seems simple enough so maybe we can all try a little harder to do that.

Meanwhile, for the time being, remaining six feet apart seems fairly *reasonable* and so you should do that as well. At some point this will become unworkable as we go back to school and lectures and seminars and public transportation etc. Therefore, at that point, if the infection rate has fallen then we should still be taking steps not to breathe on one another and so we can start shortening our distancing. It follows naturally that we will need to eventually start closing gaps and so we probably should start learning about taking reasonable steps in light of certain realities.

When it comes to cleaning and disinfecting surfaces, I say, why not? We probably should have been doing that anyway even before COVID-19. Washing your hands is not a bad idea either. Once again, that is probably something that we should have been doing before.

At some point, much like the boy in the plastic bubble, we all crave human contact and genuine forms of interaction. Virtual anything is okay but if virtual was as good as the real thing then nothing would be real anymore. So, it only makes sense that you, in your business, would opt for actual forms of interaction as opposed to merely meeting over a video link. You would rather have people being served in the ambience of your restaurant as opposed to taking the experience of your cuisine home with them where you cannot observe their reaction. You would rather physically hand something to a customer for his or her inspection than have to describe it ad nauseam on a web page.

The truth is that we all want to interact without being frightened to death that the way we used to do things will only infect and potentially kill people. So despite what we want, we need to take precautions.

However, just because we are taking the precautions prescribed by the alleged "experts" that does not mean that those are the only ways of being cautious. We have all observed the incredible creativity that the crisis has brought out in our businesspeople. Clear plastic walls have been erected over nearly every cash register in areas with higher population density. People are developing all sorts of ways of conducting business and keeping people safe. It is said that necessity is the mother of invention. In this case, innovation is certainly a favorite son. Our businesses are taking steps to do what is necessary to stay in business while also taking precautions. No one is necessarily throwing caution to the wind but we are instead finding new and creative ways of interacting safely. This is the very essence of being in business and our business owners and their crews are to be applauded for those efforts.

As we said in the first chapter, there is a lot about this coronavirus that we do not know. The extent to which it is contagious seems well settled but even that has not been established with an exact degree of certainty. As a result, an abundance of caution is probably not a bad thing. Nevertheless, reasonable people can certainly agree that even caution does not have to be taken to the extreme. We need to strike a compromise based on what we actually know and distinguish it from what seems to be the case based only on conjecture.

Our natural tendency is to do things as we always have and to question the imposition of restrictions on how we do business. This is as important now as it ever has been because as we learn the facts about the virus we need to look at whether new forms of regulation make sense or are simply over the top and unnecessary. To the extent that any of the regulations imposed by various governmental authorities are nothing more than pandemic paranoia, we need to investigate their necessity and potentially prove what is unnecessary. We need to fight regulations that are overly burdensome and not likely to prevent any actual threat.

Dare I say that we need to find some form

of compromise? As you operate your business you have to rationalize everything that you do that would otherwise interfere with the free and uninhibited exercise of your rights as a capitalist. So long as you look at things objectively then you should be willing to trust your own judgment.

Moreover, like anything else, businesspeople need to do cost benefit analysis over types of precautions to implement in doing business. A couple of boxes of gloves and masks for the staff may not be a big deal and so that might be worth the investment. A major air purifier might be overly expensive and unnecessary so that is probably not worth it.

Finally, find ways to portray your business as taking precautions seriously without adding to the fear being promulgated on the general public. Tell your clients and customers that you are taking reasonable steps but do not meet everybody at the door in a hazmat suit. The misinformation about the virus is causing enough anxiety without you adding to it. Demonstrate to your customers and clients that you appreciate that a *reasonable* response to the crisis is appropriate. Let them know that you are being both responsible and rational in taking precautions and your customers and clients will likely thank you for it. Some will scoff at it and some will feel that it is not enough. Just the same, for your purposes, show them the qualities of reasonable compromise and how you embrace that concept and most will appreciate it.

## Chapter 3
## Strategy # 3: Know Who to Blame. (Hint: It's Everybody!)

*Dr. Anthony Fauci seems to be a very nice older gentleman who is mild mannered and undoubtedly good intentioned. However, in the minds of some people, that is not likely to prevent his name from becoming a verb. Here is an exchange between two young men talking about a one's recent date:*

   George: *So we get back to her apartment and things seem like they are going in the right direction. So, she asks me if I want a drink and then invites me to sit down. So, I sit down on the sofa expecting her to sit next to me when all of a sudden . . . . she sits on a chair no closer than six feet from me! I mean c'mon . . . what did she think that we could do six feet apart?*

Jerry: *So, she Faucied you?*

George: *Yeah, that's it exactly Jerry. I got Faucied! I couldn't believe it. There's this beautiful woman who seemed receptive to me and then she decides that she wants no contact. We didn't even shake hands! I'll probably never shake hands with her - or anything else!*

To a very great extent many federal, state and local leaders are now paying the price for having been as political and divisive as they have been in the past. Many state governors are attempting to impose restrictions that a growing number of their constituents are beginning to question. These leaders have so often acted as purely political animals as to render anyone skeptical as to whether they are doing what is right as opposed to what is best for themselves politically. People are questioning whether their leaders are acting out of what is best for the public or what is best for the leader and his or her political party.

As the crisis has gone on and in the wake of the havoc it has wreaked on the economy, people are floating conspiracy theories that some local leaders are using the pandemic to score political points against the current administration regardless of what it is doing to those out of work and potentially out of business in the future. For the sake of all of us, we need to hope that there is nothing to this school of thought. However, the fact that it is being considered says a lot about our current political climate. It suggests that some politicians are so driven by their own agendas as to sacrifice countless thousands of people and their livelihoods for the sake of undoing the 2016 election. Given the rhetoric that has been spewed by these politicians in the past and the occasional jabs that they have taken at the administration in the wake of the pandemic, one can see why people are considering these conspiracies. Because these politicians cannot help themselves in attempting to score political points, they fail to focus on the fact that the virus is the enemy. People notice this and then that undermines the politician's credibility when he or she looks to impose costly and in some cases devastating restrictions.

Worse yet, some of these leaders have used the tired old political strategy of passing the buck in order to cover up for their own incompetence in the wake of the pandemic. Here is a news flash for everybody. It is so evident as to appear to be more fact than merely an opinion. Brace yourselves because it is pretty stark in the depth of its meaning. Here it is:

> In the wake of the COVID-19 pandemic and in the development of a response and in its implementation, the world has been proven completely inept!

There it is in a nutshell. Everybody has been proven incompetent in the wake of the pandemic. No one has handled it perfectly. It is not merely my bad or his bad or her bad or your bad or their bad but it is everybody's bad!

How can I say that? Well, certainly no one can say that anyone was properly prepared for this particular coronavirus. We knew about it in 2019 hence the "-19" in its name yet back in 2019 we were not getting ready for it. Basically, if we equate being prepared with having at least some idea what to do, then it is pretty clear that we were unprepared for COVID-19.

Moreover, the people who everyone thought should know what to do, the so called "experts," did not know and still do not seem to know what to do. If this was indeed a war against the coronavirus then our military strategists have been proven wrong time and time again. The truth is that the experts have failed in virtually every one of their predictions. Many of them said it was not going to be a big deal at first and we do not have to lock down the country. They told us not to overreact. Then, when it got here and started to spread, they told us that overreacting was the only way to fight it. They then forecast that it would affect and kill many millions of people which thankfully is far more than it has. Then they said that there would not be enough hospital beds and not enough respirators. Then, after retooling our industries to make respirators, they said that we do not need nearly that many. We reconstructed hospitals and moved in the *USS Comfort* and then the beds went unused. First they said we do not need masks then they said we did. To date, these folks have not gotten any prediction or statistical model right and yet they are still being touted as "experts." It is like going to the racetrack and having a guy pick the losing horse race after race and then telling everyone he is the best handicapper you have got. We have to face it. The experts have been incompetent!

And, much like the virus, the incompetence spreads as the experts advise our federal, state and local leaders. The leaders then make wrong decisions based on wrong assumptions causing more problems. And what do these political animals do when they make a mistake? They shift the blame rather than admit the mistake and rather than concede their own incompetence. The local governors blame the federal response. Worse yet, some of the local leaders throw the public under the bus by railing on about how we are not properly social distancing and congregating etc. To these leaders all I can say is "excuse us but this is our first pandemic and we all seem to be learning as we go along!"

And so as not to feel left out, with all due respect, all the rest of us have been incompetent in the wake of the pandemic and the response! To our credit, inasmuch as we have taken precautions and agreed to stay at home and wear masks and social distance, we are the least guilty of incompetence based on following others' incompetence but still this is on us too. We were not prepared mentally, physically or financially. This thing hit and a lot of us are screwed. They say that luck favors the prepared and in this case we pressed our luck!

So, despite rampant incompetence by everyone, politicians have chosen to simply shift the blame from themselves to everyone else. In doing so, they show no humility in being wrong. Those who are never blameworthy are never leaders, they are merely posers. Humility is an essential character trait of all good leaders.

Now, to be fair, the real incompetence by *ALL* of us can be summed as a failure of imagination. It seems that despite all the shows about Armageddon and zombies walking the earth, we failed to be able to perceive and react to even a mere taste of Armageddon. We did not see this coming and we were not prepared, Shame on all of us!

Finally, some leaders have utilized the political strategy of debasing those who oppose them by suggesting false equivalencies to attack their detractors. They accuse those who question their restrictions of allegedly killing people. They say things like, "I say we keep the economy shut down and if you don't like it then you support killing people." Or, they imply, "if all you care about is saving your businesses then you don't care about the people who will die from the virus if they become infected after we restart the economy." To them it is all or nothing as to embracing their unilateral edicts on wearing masks and social distancing. They are implying that if you are "pro-business" then you do not care about those who are infected and dying. Some go so far as to blame your mere act of questioning them for additional unspecified deaths. This is despicable.

For your purposes as a businessperson, avoid getting caught up in the blame game. Everyone in this instance is to blame so it makes no sense to blame anyone else or anyone in particular. Lacking humility at this particular juncture is not going to do any good. Passing the buck is not going to do any good. Sheltering in our individual political camps is not going to do any good.

Rather than play the blame game, we need to clean up the mess, learn from our mistakes, and expand our imaginations to be prepared for what might happen in the future. It really is that simple. Spending time assessing blame is pointless. Moving on is all that matters now.

And as some of my colleagues in the legal profession sharpen their wingtips in anticipation for the lawsuits that they will file against everybody in the wake of this mess, perhaps they should consider that their actions actually inhibit our ability to cope in these situations. If all we ever do is threaten to sue everybody for everything then no one will want to do anything. We will inadvertently stifle the very ingenuity that we might need to get us out of this mess. We cannot attach liability to every experiment that could potentially make things better. If no one will take a risk for fear of getting sued then bold and necessary experimentation will be inhibited.

So for now, if anyone asks you "who is to

blame for this?" then you can answer simply, "who cares." The failure in this instance can be shared universally. Finger pointing is a waste of energy. There is no point in trying to determine who got us here. We are here. Now it is time to get to where we want to be. That is a business perspective that will serve you well.

## Chapter 4
## Strategy # 4: Businesses Are All in this Together

*I'm sorry but I have a hard time listening to celebrities claim that we are "all in this together." When they are taking a selfie at home in a house that has more square footage than any building I will ever step inside in my whole life, then I can safely say that we just do not relate.*

Back in Chapter 1 we called the crisis a "mess." When you think of this as a mess then it becomes somewhat easier to put into perspective. We determine that all any business owner can do is clean up the mess as it affects your business and then just keeping plugging away. Much like if a tree falls across several properties you need to clear it from your property. If you have some energy left after clearing your property then go ahead and help your neighbors clean theirs up. Hopefully they will return the favor if it ever becomes necessary to do so in the future.

In its own way it is little more complicated than "do onto others . . ." but the principle is basically the same. Help out your fellow business people and they will probably return the favor. Or, to seem more businesslike about it, invest in helping others and they should be willing to invest in you.

The business landscape in the wake of the pandemic is likely to be fairly sparse. The chances of a quick turnaround seem remote. Instinctively it is a time when most would think it best to adopt the motto: every man for himself. Yet, as we get ready to reopen and navigate beyond this mess it is more likely the best time to help your fellow man any way that you can. We will have to count on one another.

As independent businesspeople, naturally this seems contrary to our basic instinct. Independence and self-reliance have always been two of the fundamental tenets of business. In normal times when things are moderate to good then independence can be a rational strategy. However, in times like what we are facing now, we have no choice but to rely upon one another. We need to strengthen our networking and do as much cross promoting as possible.

Cross promoting? The phrase might be new but the concept should not be. The truth is that we can help our fellow business owners by making referrals and doing some incidental advertising for them as often as we can without seeming like a shill.

It often happens that in the course of seeking opportunities for yourself you end up finding work that needs to be done by someone else. The guy going door to door offering estimates to fix sidewalks and driveways will often come across folks needing a new roof. If you know of a good roofer then put the property owner in touch with the roofer. Chances are, if the roofer is looking for work, he or she may come across a guy who needs a new sidewalk.

Talk to people and see what they need. If they do not need your services then see if there is anything else that they need and make a personal recommendation. Word of mouth referrals are projected in the smallest increments but are by far and away the most persuasive. Tell someone you have a good plumber and you will be referring him or her to everybody. When you get your plumber friend a job then be ready to tell him or her to make sure that they know what you do.

If a fellow business owner is having an open house to celebrate reopening then do your best to attend. Do what you can to create a buzz for your fellow businesses. Make them look successful and it will make you seem successful.

And, despite your sense of purely self-reliance, be willing to accept help from your fellow business owners when they send work your way. Show enthusiasm for what they can refer to you. There is nothing wrong with having someone else promote you. Good free publicity is always worth more than you pay for it and likely more than you would have paid.

In times like these, looking out for the other guy is not a worn out cliche but is instead a strategy that usually pays dividends. Perhaps it is Karma or just plain luck but usually helping others, especially when times get tough, helps you in the long run. It gives you something to do. It allows you to think a little less about your own troubles. It makes you feel good.

The point is that we need solidarity as businesses. Help one another out. Nothing against Amazon but if you can help out a small business that does not actively use the internet then throw some business their way. Otherwise, remember that Amazon is a platform for selling from businesses and so you should look to support businesses that are selling to you through Amazon too.

And, perhaps as important as any other aspect to helping others is the tendency it has to prevent feelings of loneliness for both the helper and the helped. There is no point to remaining isolated at this particular time. So far as I know, you cannot contract the virus via phone interactions so put a call out to your fellow businesspeople. Do what you can to help the other guy to pull out of this. Being a part of another guy's success will help you feel that you are at least a part of something. From a purely mental perspective, this is not a good time to be an island.

## Chapter 5
## Strategy # 5: Disinfect

*Anyone who serves as the Surgeon General usually wears a uniform with a bunch of medals across the chest and so I had to wonder, what are they for? If he or she were to brag about them would they say something like, "oh this one, I got that bad boy in the battle of herpes. I actually have three of those medals because you end up having to fight that battle again and again."*

While businesses are closed and while people are home, things can become a little lax. There is a tendency to let things go. A little bit of laziness creeps in as we are forced to remain idle by our COVID care-taking overlords. Meanwhile, as some of us are still working, we watch those who are not and we become ever so resentful. Perhaps, we even become jealous. We yearn to feel as free as they obviously feel in getting caught up on binge watching *Star Trek* in all of its various incarnations.

We would certainly welcome more work and in some cases we actually have more work to do but still we see others obviously carefree and enjoying their time off and we ask: "why can't I take it easy?"

In some instances, you are at work and there is not much to do. The shutdown has slowed business to a crawl and we find ourselves clock watching. Sure there are things that we *could* do but we just do not seem to find the time to *want* to do them.

Mental meandering becomes a problem. We daydream away the hours without focus and without purpose. Productivity becomes almost completely lost. Your business starts to look about as overdue for a haircut as you do.

Speaking metaphorically, your business is suffering from some of the less than obvious symptoms of the virus. Your efficiency and determination are affected. Your business is suffering the more tangential aspects of being afflicted with COVID - 19.

So, before you let the virus take hold and otherwise shut you down to any extent, this may be a good time to disinfect your business. Clean it up. Make it ready. Do the things that you always wish you had time to do but do not seem to ever get around to doing. Read articles about new ways of marketing. Read about market trends, Read the *Wall Street Journal* and *Investors' Business Daily*. Read this book - it was fairly cheap!

During your working hours devote your time and full attention to doing business. Balance the checkbook. Install software updates. Prepare databases and draft newsletters. Do an inventory. Clean the carpets, dust the shelves, get rid of the old magazines in the lobby, swap out some of the pictures throughout the office.

Tidy up your website and make sure that it is up to date. Review your phone and internet bills. Comparison shop your utilities, insurance and other miscellaneous expenses.

Basically, the point is that you need to

keep busy. Your business might be on the sideline but there is still a chance that you may get in the game soon. Be ready! Look busy. Be busy. And to the extent that you can, feel busy.

The virus may indirectly usher in a sense of malaise. Do not let that consume you. Do whatever you need to do to stay engaged. Do whatever it takes to project your business as being very healthy and alive. That will give customers and clients a sense of satisfaction just knowing that somebody is coping with the crisis. They will find it reassuring that your business is immune to the crisis. They will see your business as a bastian of normalcy in a sea of uncertainty. This will make them feel a distinct sense of calm that will continue to attract your regular customers and will appeal to those who will be getting to know you.

The point is to demonstrate that despite all that is happening, your business maintains its steadiness and health. Your business will be affected and there is nothing wrong with conceding that but try to portray it as strong regardless of the pandemic. Ancient constructions will show signs of deteriorating but the pillars will withstand the test of time. Be the pillars.

The pathway to everyone getting back to how things were before runs through those things that are immune to the virus. The ones who will lead us down that path are those who have stayed focused and avoided any sense of quitting or even relaxing in the face of getting us back on track. Those are the businesses that will be poised to thrive in the post COVID-19 world!

## Chapter 6
## Strategy # 6: Lifelines

*It is said that there is nothing to lose in helping others because even though goodness is not always contagious and good deeds seldom go unpunished, you may inadvertently help someone who wins the lottery some day. Then, they may repay your kindness. And if they don't then you have the satisfaction of being able to say, "sure they've got money but that doesn't make them any less of an asshole!" So, at least that is something.*


God bless the memory of the *RMS Carpathia*. Few might recall that *Carpathia* was the steamer that came to the rescue of the survivors after the sinking of the *Titanic*. It seems ironic that so many remember the name of the iceberg's victim but few recall the name of the hero in the story. People remember the name of Rose and Jack and they were not even real.

Nonetheless, if ever there was a time for businesses to be heros for one another it is right now! The knee-jerk decision to virtually unplug the economy and send everyone home hit many small businesses much like the iceberg hit the Titanic. Few had time to properly prepare and even fewer had the capacity to react before the economy started sinking. In the wake of the economy splitting apart and heading to the bottom, a number of small businesses are left scattered in tiny lifeboats a drift in the ocean and seemingly without hope of any imminent rescue.

The analogies do not stop there. The economy, much like the Titanic, did not have enough lifeboats for all businesses to survive. It was an economy that much like the Titanic was considered unsinkable. It had been humming along. It was the pride of the world. It was an accomplishment of great importance. Certainly, it could race through an ice field without consequence.

Moreover, engineers and ship architects familiar with the Titanic's potential to be "unsinkable" have theorized that had the Titanic simply run into the iceberg and not attempted to avoid it that perhaps it would not have sunk. If the Titanic would have hit the iceberg head on then only the bow might have been severely damaged but the ship itself may have remained afloat. The act of changing course so suddenly however caused the iceberg to rip a hole along side the watertight chambers in the hull such that water eventually filled a sufficient amount of the individual chambers which spilled over each of the bulkheads so as to tear the ship in half and sink her.

Likewise, there is a theory that perhaps had we not necessarily have tried to avoid the pandemic and allowed some level of herd immunity to develop then perhaps it would not have sunk the economy. This may have caused more deaths at the time of the initial outbreak but less over time and perhaps the economy would not have tanked. It is merely a theory however and, much like what happened with the

Titanic, we will never know what could have been.

What we do know is that there are a lot of businesses affected and likely to die as a result of what we did do. Many of our local leaders have been no more steady than the crew of the Titanic who tried to shuffle half empty lifeboats full of little businesses to the water. Declaring some businesses as necessary and others not was like marshaling first and then second class passengers to boats and basically treating other businesses like steerage that could go down with the economy.

So, in an attempt to state the obvious once again to the point of reiterating it ad nauseam, we were not prepared and now we have a mess!

Whatever we could have done with regard to how we reacted to the pandemic as it made its way to America is spilled milk that we cannot waste time crying over. What is done is done and now we have to turn our attention to the rescue mission. The ship that was the economy has broken in two and no one can stay aboard it so as to survive. Our small businesses are in lifeboats.

Those ships that have remained afloat must now lend a hand in the rescue efforts. Much like the *RMS Carpathia*, businesses that have been able to navigate through the ice field need to rescue those businesses in the lifeboats. Businesses that are able must pluck their fellow businesses out of the near frozen waters and give them shelter and passage back to land.

Now as most people know, the *RMS Carpathia* did not sink in rescuing the survivors of the Titanic. Similarly, the businesses that are surviving the pandemic do not have to risk sinking in order to rescue the small businesses they will find. Instead, we merely need to help these businesses any way that we can. For instance, if you can buy something from a struggling business then go ahead and buy it. If the restaurant is offering curbside pickups and take out and you can afford it then order all that you can. If a company is making something that you could otherwise buy online then buy it direct from the small company.

Moreover, if you can put small businesses

that are still afloat in touch with other people who could use their products or services then do it. What I advised in Chapter 4 bears repeating. If you can help your fellow business owners then do so. Make introductions. Help them network. The only way to actually "all be in this together" is to be able to communicate amongst ourselves. Get people in business in touch with one another.

The point is this, establish lifelines to the businesses that are attempting to survive in the wake of COVID-19. Do not risk your own health but help your fellow business if you are able. No order is too small to save a business. Maybe you cannot buy the whole car but you could still get the oil changed. Maybe you cannot afford a total remodel but you could get the place painted. If you need business cards then if you cannot afford 10,000 then at least order 1,000.

And, for what it is always worth, do some incidental advertising for one another. Tell everyone you can get to listen about the plumbing service who handle a project for you.

Make sure the plumber mentions how your store sells the best produce. Mention how good your CPA is or the positive experience you had with your dentist. Make certain that they tell people what a great contractor you are. Bring your winter coats to the dry cleaners who have not been pressing suits for a while because no one goes to the office anymore. While you are there, ask them if you can leave a tray of cookies alongside your business cards in their window to promote your bakery.

    We need to throw those lifelines to one another. Slowly, we can help each other get from the lifeboats to the shore.

## Chapter 7
## Strategy # 7: Apolitical to the End

*Because of the lock-down this year, rather than attend church, I simply binge watched an internet broadcast of the Stations of the Cross on Good Friday. Spoiler alert: the Main Character dies in episode 12 but they set it up so that He would have a miraculous return three days later for season 2.*

Politicians have seldom solved any problem. Politics solves fewer problems still. And, for your purposes as a business person, being political has never solved a problem. For businesses, there is little or nothing to be gained from acting politically in a crisis. Pledging allegiance to one side or the other of the political spectrum has never been the move that saved or even benefitted a business. For example, there is this company whose symbol is a swoosh that continues to promote a political activist who masquerades as a football player. Regardless of whether one agrees with the guy or not, he engages in actions that some people find offensive. Some of those people, as you might imagine, are likely in the shoe buying demographic. So, I could be wrong but one would think that giving the guy a forum to continue to be political probably did not sell a lot of shoes for the swoosh and might have actually lost a great number of customers.

Controversy does not always result in higher sales and is a relatively risky marketing strategy. Generally speaking, the only thing that being political ever does is give some people a reason not to like you. In business, this is never a good thing.

When it comes to politics, the best policy for a businessperson is to be above it. This is easy to do because politicians so often act like arrested adolescents that it provides businesspeople with ample opportunity to appear mature by contrast. While politicians spar and fight over petty inconsequential differences you can focus on what is really important.

You can have your own political opinions of course but as a businessperson it is best to keep those opinions to yourself. No one needs to know your political opinion of anything because that opinion is not important to what your stand for in business.

You can have your own principles. If a particular politician embraces those principles then give him or her a gentle nod without specifically endorsing them. For instance, you can say something like, "the President said that he hopes that the economy will come roaring back and I for one hope that he is right." Is this political? Not necessarily because you are not endorsing anything other than a hope for a good outcome. Anyone who would attack this sentiment is being political however because to hope that things go badly only serves those who are out of power.

When it comes right down to it, you cannot become preoccupied with all the bickering and back-stabbing in Washington D.C. or in your state's capital or even in your hometown local leadership. We can hope and pray that our leaders have everyone's best interests in mind but some probably do not. Some are good people and fair-minded leaders and others are just political hacks. All of them have their hands full right now and there is no way of knowing how it will all shake out. Some will win in the end and some will lose. Public opinion will move back and forth and some will show genuine leadership while others will fail to espouse the qualities that we wish they had.

Moreover, in the wake of the pandemic, there is nothing to be gained by espousing an opinion on either the seriousness of the virus or the nature of the response. Some people are scared to death of the disease and are taking it very seriously perhaps to the point of being obsessed. Some are profoundly casual about it and do not think that it is any big deal. Frankly, this is somewhat another form of politics in that different people maintain significantly different feelings about the pandemic and the response.

There is no point in seeming insensitive to the ones who are taking it seriously and there is nothing to be gained by attempting to urge others to take it more seriously. You may feel one way or the other and that is fine. However, your business is a distinct entity from you and when it comes to the pandemic and the response, your business should have no opinion.

For your purposes as you deal with all of the opinions and politics, it might be best to just let it all go. Do not back one person or another. Do not back one party or the other. Do not take the virus too seriously but do not blow it off. Do not judge those who are in panic mode or those who could not care less. Do not let your business's opinion get put "on the record' so to speak. There is no point in picking horses in a race where you have nothing to win by betting.

The guiding principle for your business when it comes to being political is how to have the most people maintain a positive impression of you and it. If you cannot obtain a positive impression from others then you must do what you can to have people maintain a neutral impression of you. Do not let people think, "well, he supports so and so and I do not like so and so and therefore I will not do business with him." Do not let them think, "she feels that I am not taking the whole thing seriously just because I do not wear a mask everywhere I go." If you are thought to have picked a side then those on the other side will have a reason not to look upon you favorably. You can do business with people who like you. You can do business with people who are indifferent to you. But, you will not do much business with people who hate you for no other reason than your political leanings. So when it comes to maintaining one's appeal in business, always remember, it is best never to give a potential customer a reason to dislike you.

    People will sometimes seek your political opinion or your opinion about the pandemic perhaps even just for the sake of making conversation. They may attempt to goad you into demonstrating what you like or which side of the aisle you support. Do not trap yourself merely for the sake of small talk. Find ways to discreetly move the topic onto something else. In the midst of the current economic situation there is no problem in simply conceding, "you know, all the political stuff is for people who have time to analyze it but as for me, I'm just worried about making sure that I'm keeping my customers happy." There is a good reason to say this because in the end, this is what your focus should be!

Our country is very divided. Who cares? You have a business to run. One party or the other is handling things poorly. Who cares? You have a business to run. Some politicians are doing a great job. Who cares? You have a business to run. Some are doing a terrible job. Who cares? You have a business to run. This guy or that girl is an idiot. Who cares? You have a business to run. This politician is incompetent. Who cares? You have a business to run. This guy or girl is a socialist. Who cares? You have a business to run. This guy or girl is a true patriot. Who cares? You have a business to run.

The pandemic will result in the end of human beings. Okay, but you have a business to run. The pandemic is a government plot to take away our liberty. Okay, but you have got a business to run. The people who are not staying home are risking the lives of countless millions. Okay, but you have a business to run. The people who are reporting their neighbors for congregating in their own yards and using the grill are being extreme. Okay, but you have a business to run.

The point is simply this: whatever political stripes you adopt should have little bearing on your business. Your business should be apolitical because in the end we have a crisis. The last thing that your business wants to do in the midst of a crisis is to alienate anyone. Your business should be willing to portray itself as a place where anyone with any political affiliation can do business. Let everyone know that regardless of what they espouse politically, your business will treat them indiscriminately. Let them know that your business is a safe harbor from the turbulent seas of political divisiveness. This will do a lot of good for your customers and it might just help you as well. Your business might be the one place where you come in from the political storms outside.

## Chapter 8
## Strategy # 8: Dealing with the Big Boys

*One day while I was in the office a friend asked what I was doing and I told him that I was writing a disclaimer for a placebo commercial. I explained how I was up to the part about side effects . . .*

*" . . You may drink alcohol while taking placebo, kiddie cocktails and near beer go especially well with it . . .*
*. . If you experience an erection lasting in excess of four hours while taking placebo then call your doctor immediately and brag about it!"*

Many can recall from back in the late

1960's and early 1970's when the youth movement proudly shouted their decree: "don't trust anyone over 30." It was as if at 30 years of age people suddenly woke up to all the realities of life that were not readily apparent to arrested adolescent Baby Boomers. People in their 30's did things like raised families and held jobs and paid taxes so that states could provide universities for Baby Boomers to tear up with their protests that did nothing really other than prolong the Vietnam War because the Baby Boomers could not rationally express themselves and merely vilified the older generation and affixed the moniker "establishment" on them like that was some evil empire thing like the one in *Star Wars* which movie seems to have officially marked the end of the radical days of the 1960's and 70's by empowering geeks. But, I digress . . .

The Baby Boomers told their ranks that trusting people who surpassed the age of 30 was bad. There was even a movie about a future world where everyone over 30 was systematically murdered by the government. The movie was *Logan's Run* and it featured Farrah Faucett. For the uniformed or otherwise uninitiated, may I suggest Googling: Farrah, swimsuit poster.

Anyway, with a nod to the Baby Boomers' decree, the new mantra for small business should be: "don't trust any business with over 30 (employees)!" Then I thought about it and although it works symmetrically with 60's thing, 30 is probably too small a number. Even with 30 employees a business can be actually somewhat small. Perhaps some of those employees are part-timers. That would skew the number significantly. I considered suggesting: "don't trust any company with over 300 (employees)." Then, as I thought about it some more, I realized that 300 seemed like too many (unless of course you are Spartans at Thermopylae taking on 70,000 Persians). I did determine that I like the parenthesis around "employees" however. Nonetheless, 300 was too many. Maybe 100 works. Let's try: "don't trust any company with over 100 (employees)." Now I am questioning the parenthesis on the "employees." . . . .

This much thought on my part may undermine my point. So, think about this. Big companies stick it to small companies all the time. They bully us and treat us like crap without a second thought. They take advantage when they can and they have no sense of sympathy. Many are unethical in their dealings and they simply could care less if you call them on it. They prize profit over honor and if they gave any thought to small business at all then they would at least look down on us. Sadly, they do not even do that.

Believe it or not, I am not saying that this is a bad thing or that Big Business is necessarily bad. They do some very important things and they accomplish goals that we small businesses could not for lack of resources and a more vast pool of talent. Some who run big businesses are genuine in their desire to improve the world although their vision of its betterment is skewed by their own sense of righteousness. Nevertheless, to be fair, some big businesses can do great things.

Despite some of their noble achievements however big businesses are more or less the spoiled children of our economy. They get their way and cry (and sue) if they do not. They mistreat others without remorse, and worse yet, without repercussions. They get away with a lot as they maintain a sense that none of us could live without them. About this, they may be right but then again, for our part, we learn to live without each of them eventually. After all, how many of the Fortune 500 in 1950 were still on that list in 2000? Or, when did you last go shopping in a Sears department store? Do you want a stock tip? Keep an eye on your cable companies. In the not so distant future they are going to be about as prosperous as someone opening a Blockbuster video franchise. Could it be that 75 ohm cable is the buggy whip of current technology? *And in those dreams whatever they be, stream a little stream of me.*

In any event, the point is that big businesses are in the business of staying big. No one should fault them for this. It is what they are all about and if you know that going in then you can prepare yourself for dealing with them. Do not delude yourself into thinking that they will help you. They will not even play fair (ask Preston Tucker). Big businesses can pull strings that you could never see. They can wield influence that you never knew existed. They have considerable power even in times marked by the likes of COVID-19.

So, when you see their commercials telling you how big businesses are trying to be sympathetic, do not fall for it. These are PR campaigns intent on making the general public not distrust them quite so much.

But, for you in your small business, I suggest that you go right on distrusting them. They could not possibly give less of a crap about whether you make it or not so do not fall for them telling you that "we are all in this together." That is a crock of crap. When the boat that is the economy starts to go down, big business will push us little guys over the side like we were bad smelling fish just to get to the life boats. They are bastards. Crisis or not, they could not give a damn about your small business unless it can help their bottom line somehow. And then they only value you for what you can do for them. As I said, "bastards."

Will big businesses let me get away with this? Probably. You see, I am no big deal to them. They have about as much respect for my opinions as my kids do. As insignificant as I am there is little that I can do to get their attention other than to perhaps miss a payment. Skipping a payment usually gets one noticed by big business. It puts one on their radar. It makes one worthy of a phone call from them. Otherwise, as long as us small fish stay obedient and servile, big business does not even know that we are here.

What will happen when this book catches on and people start reading this chapter? Big business will not care because they still have the power. Even though I will have made you aware of their great power and influence, it is of no consequence. What does it matter to them that you are aware of their great power so long as you can do nothing to limit that power? Telling a spoiled child that you are aware that they are spoiled does not make them behave any better. They simply say, "you're aware that I'm spoiled well then good for you, now get me that toy!"

So, for your purposes in small business as you arm yourselves to handle the fallout imposed by our political overlords who threw us into the COVID-19 chaos, what you need to do is be aware of what Big Business is all about. They do not care about you. Do you want to know how you can be sure of that? Tell them that you read this book and they will say, "don't listen to that asshole." That is how you will know that some pimp who works for a Big Business is about to stick it to you. You see, they will tell you that I am the asshole for saying what I wrote in this book but they will act like they are a hero for letting you renew your internet contract for two years at a special COVID-19 rate. Compare the cover price of this book to what a Big Business will directly debit from your account each month for the next 24 months and then you tell me who the "asshole" is.

Should you deal with Big Business? Yup.

You really do not have a choice. They own and operate a lot of what you need in your small business. You cannot ignore them. You need banks to hold your money and your stuff to be delivered. You need an internet platform to buy things and you need some asshole company to provide internet service. You need your phones to work and you need your lights to go on. The truth is: Big Business plops its ass in your face every day and you have no choice but to kiss it! Don't be ashamed. We all do it. We all have to do it. Every prostitute is an entrepreneur and every entrepreneur is . . . .

I guess that some of us would like to think that if we ran a big business then we would be better. Who knows? Frankly speaking, who cares? If you make it big then be whatever and whoever you are. If you are a good person then continue to be a good person. You can be both good and successful. Decency may be an impediment to acquiring wealth but it is not necessarily a prerequisite to never attaining it.

For your purposes as you try to survive as a small business in a big crisis, you merely need to realize that big businesses are not your friends who are worried about your little bait shop. They are not losing sleep over whether you can make payroll or rent his week. If you go broke then you are of even less importance to them than usual (if that is possible). Otherwise, they do not see your problems as being of particular importance to them.

So, deal with Big Business with this in mind. If you can make a buck selling to them then do it. Make them pay you on time however because whenever you think you can make a buck dealing with them you usually end up with only about 70¢. Do not let them cheat you, do not try to be their friend (other than to their face) and do not rely upon Big Business as the catalyst that will make this nightmare end. They are not invested in you so do not get sucked into investing too heavily in them. Let them make a profit and do not forget that you are trying to do the same thing.

And, if a decision comes down to doing something that benefits you versus benefitting some big business then put yourself in their shoes and ask what they would do for you. Seems selfish? Sure, I guess. So if it makes you feel better, stick it to some big company and then write them a pithy little note thanking them for their business and letting them know that "we are all in this together!"

## Chapter 9
## Strategy # 9: Know Who to Trust

*A rabbi walks into a bar and says . . .*
*Nope, I can't make fun of rabbis. Let's try again.*
*A priest walks into a bar and says . . .*
*Nope, that might be offensive. Let's try again.*
*A Muslin cleric walks into a bar . . .*
*No way I'm not going there. Let's try again.*
*A transvestite walks into a bar . . . .*
*Nope, definitely not. Let's try again.*
*A white guy walks into a bar and just before he gets ready to speak, the bartender says, "hey pal are you from the CDC?"*
*"No," the man answers somewhat confused by the question.*
*"Well then I can't serve you because we're closed by order of the*

*governor."*

*"Sorry to hear that," the patron says.*

*"And, if you don't mind . . ." the bartender begins a request, "could you please tell the rabbi, the priest, the Muslim cleric and the transvestite out in front that I was not trying to be politically correct? It's just that the bar is closed because of COVID-19 and I can't serve them. I can't even let them in for a joke!"*


I have said it several times to this point. We are a country divided. Frankly, we are a world divided. Over the last several years and perhaps decades we have become so devoted to what we individually believe that we only tend to listen and associate with those who think like us. We gravitate toward people of certain political stripes with whom we are more prone to agree.

Moreover, we have come to dismiss those with whom we disagree. For the most part, we tune them out. When we do listen then we attempt to cling to something they might have said so as to poke wholes in their argument or their point of view. We characterize them as anything from merely "out of touch" to total idiots. We disregard any logical arguments that they might have made and we belittle them and those who think like them. They resent us for deigning to disagree with them and they reassemble with their cohorts so as to poke fun at us and the cycle repeats itself over and over to the point that we remain . . . . divided.

Being divided in this way may not necessarily be problematic when things are good. I do not mean to suggest that it is healthy for the world to be so divided but when times are good so long as the bickering does not become outright violent then it is relatively innocuous.

The problem with being so divided is when it occurs during periods of crisis and when things are no so good. When people's lives and livelihoods are at risk then being divided creates a more significant problem for us. It is at those times that we may need to pull together or at least form some element of consensus about some important issues.

    We came together that after the 9/11 attacks. There was a strong sense of unity in the country. First responders and police and firemen were heralded by just about everyone as heros at the time. We developed a respect for certain institutions and despite the wound inflicted by a third party, we relied upon one another to heal our nation and to implement ways to protect ourselves together.

    Then, over time, our divisiveness reared its ugly head as we resorted to the old blame game. Politics seeped into the matter as some people with various agendas started to seek opportunities to score political points. The 9/11 attacks started to slide ever so slightly into our collective rearview mirrors and we became divided once again. Various incidents occurred involving individuals of one color or another, or involving the police or involving truly evil or sick people. Those who are feeding our division use those incidents as examples to indict entire sections of the populace. Riots emerge as if we are waxing nostalgic for the tumultuousness of the 1960's. Those intent on our remaining divided pedal untrue stereotypes on the presumption that all cops are bad and all white people are racists and all heterosexual men are rapists and all women are subjugated and minorities are subordinated etc.

Politicians play upon the self-imposed victimhood that some folks begin to feel much like the lawyers who advertise on late night televisions that they will gladly handle your personal injury case. Our divisiveness grows deeper and . . . . here is the most important part of my dissertation . . . we no longer trust one another!

Face it, regardless of where you fall politically, you do not trust the people who disagree with you when it comes to major issues. When it comes to the coronavirus and the response, no one seems to trust anyone from the other side. Some people think that the overreaction to the virus might have been created for no other reason than to derail the current administration. Others feel that reopening the economy is being done with a complete disregard for those dying from the disease so as to help the administration in an election year.

Then the media jumps in on their high horse of self importance and complete lack of journalistic integrity to weigh in on the side of those who support their agenda. As a result of being blinded by their own sense of self-righteousness, the media no longer presents the news but instead merely introduces issues it likes to promote with generally fictitious storylines to shore up their arguments. When you think about it, it is really quite despicable.

Meanwhile, as I have said time and time again, you have a business to run. In doing that, you need to rely upon certain things, For example, as we discussed in Chapter 1, you have to rely upon information. You need to learn to decipher what information is accurate and what is not. Eventually, you have to trust that the information you are relying upon is valid so as to allow you to engage in good decision-making.

Nearly as important as it is to rely upon the

validity of the information is the fact that you have to be able to rely upon people. As we touched on in Chapter 1, you need to determine who or who might not be a trustworthy source of information as you navigate through this crisis. Moreover, you will also have to actually know *who* to trust to actually help you as you try to move your business back to some level of regular existence and potential prosperity.

Knowing who to trust is tricky. It always has been and likely always will be. Add to that the current crisis and knowing who to trust becomes that much more integral to what you need to accomplish.

Time is critical in a crisis. We have less time to investigate and evaluate our options. Sometimes we have to make hasty decisions. In doing so, we sometimes need to count on others to have our backs in the event that either our decisions are wrong or if a right decision needs to be implemented. In these instances, the people you rely upon will make the difference and so you need to know who to trust.

Perhaps in determining what people are

worthy of your trust it would be easier to look at it in terms of the process of elimination. The easier question becomes: who you should not trust?

Well, as we have eluded to already, the mainstream media is not necessarily friendly to businesspeople and capitalists like yourselves. Watch them long enough and you will feel the actual disdain for you seep through their coverage of just about anything. They seem to love the people who embrace socialism which just in case you were wondering is contrary to what your business is about. The mainstream media has an agenda that they try, but fail miserably, to hide. They have very liberal tendencies rooted in the general belief that big government, when run by the elites, makes sense because the general populace is not capable of taking care of themselves. They feel that the elites in government should impose more regulations and restrictions because they know better than the masses. The media empathizes with those who are more educated and therefore presumably more intelligent than the masses.

The masses are incapable of properly governing themselves and therefore they need the elites to rule over them as gracious benefactors.

Trusting anyone who thinks that they are smarter than you is not necessarily a bad thing but trusting anyone who thinks that they are smarter than everyone is foolish. These elitist snobs in the media and in academia feel that they are superior to everyone else including businesspeople who likely have made a fortune or two without the benefit of formal education. These elitists belittle and mock small business people as quaint but otherwise lucky morons. When these small businesses enjoy some level of success these elitists contend that they did so in spite of themselves. They discount the value of both ingenuity and hard work.

So, in knowing whom to trust, you can assume that the mainstream media is not going to provide you with accurate information or genuine support. They resent your independence and feel that despite your prosperity you still require the guidance of the patronizing elitists. These folks are not invested in you taking the steps to have your business survive the crisis on your own. They would much rather see you struggle on you own without absolute authority and guidance by those elites in government and academia that they feel have all the answers.

As for the elites in government for whom the mainstream media feels so affectionate, these are the politicians who are acting as if they have absolute authority in the wake of the crisis. They have closed your businesses for your own good. They often acted contrary to the actual legal authority that they possess because they narcissistically believe that they "know better." These are the local politicians who feel that they can disregard the state constitution and the federal constitution simply because the crisis calls for people who are smarter than everyone else to rule with an iron fist. They have deemed themselves the smartest people in the room and therefore they are free to impose their will over you and everyone else because they alone know what is right.

These people cannot be trusted. They have already demonstrated that they lack any genuine concern for you and your business when they unilaterally closed you without notice, due process or even an *"I'm sorry."*

These overbearing politicians have attempted to use the "crisis" to grab incredible amounts of power. We can assume that they do not care about your opinion on the subject. Actually, given what we have seen so far in this regard, we can move that assumption from the "safe bet" to the proven fact side of our information gathering.

We addressed the idea that your business should remain apolitical in Chapter 7 but at this point, this is what you need to know about politics for the sake of navigating your business through this mess. Most politicians cannot relate to small businesses and therefore they do not give them much thought. Ironically, they tax the business entities but those entities (corporations, limited liability companies, partnerships) cannot vote. So, politicians do not seem to care about small, seemingly powerless business entities that cannot vote or otherwise influence them.

Moreover, most politicians use stereotypes

of business owners to scapegoat them for the politicians' own political purposes. They portray business owners as the "haves" and then bash on them for the sake of getting votes from the "have nots." They tell you about how businesspeople are greedy and rich and how they subjugate and abuse their employees and how the government forces businesses to pay ever higher minimum wages etc. because business owners like to underpay folks. Politicians impose regulations on businesses to force the alleged "haves" to deal fairly with the "have nots."

So what does this tell you as you try to figure out how to manage the COVID-19 crisis when it comes to your business? It tells you that politicians who run the government have nothing to lose by screwing you in this crisis. They may pay you lip service but for the most part they have little or no sympathy for you as they close you down. They are playing a percentage. More "have nots" vote than "haves" and because you are working and do not often get to the polls on election day, they serve the interests of who votes for them.

And, if you protest and express an opinion that you wish to reopen your business so as to survive, they then portray you as insensitive to the plight of the dying. They blame you for the deaths you will cause should you deign to even question whether you can open your business. They tell the "have nots" that you who had to open your business are responsible for all the deaths that followed after that.

Here is the point. Here is an assumption that seems fairly easy to prove. You are not merely fighting for the survival of your business in the wake of COVID-19. You are also fighting those politicians in government who are only too happy to use you as a strawman to enhance their own political careers. It is a myth when politicians tell you that we are all in this together. They are still going to do what is politically in their own best interests. If that means that they will close you up, throw you under the bus or vilify you and your small business then they will not hesitate. The sum net gain of everything that a narcissist claims he or she does for your benefit is still zero. It will always be zero. They only look at you in terms of your value to them and what they assume that they mean to you.

So how should you use this information? Based on what you can assume, for the sake of your business you have to realize that you cannot trust the government that had little or no compunction about closing you up. It is not good news but at least if you know it going in then you can make your decisions based on what is the reality of the situation.

So other than the mainstream media and the elitists in government, is there anyone else who you should not trust? Can you even trust your humble author, yours truly? Well, that depends. You see if you are looking for someone who cares about small businesses then I am your guy.

Anyone who reads my work would know that I have a certain political bent but that does not mean that I only care about people who agree with me. I fashion myself as a small business activist who could care less whether you, as a business owner, are liberal or conservative. I really just want your business to thrive. I want to see it come back stronger for having survived this mess. So long as you are committed to making your business work, it does not matter to me how you vote or how you think. I do not even care what you think of me or what I think. The point is that I support you and I want your business to thrive. That is what is important to me and that is the reason I wrote this book.

So what does that tell you about whom you should trust? It tells you that you can trust your employee who does not vote the same way as you do but still gets to work on time and puts in a solid effort to help your business. It tells you that your regular customer who wears a button for some political party that you find offensive but is loyal to buying from you is someone you can trust.

The people who are actually rooting for you and the people who are patronizing your business and the people who are selling to you in the hope that you will keep buying from them and the people who work for you because they know that you have their back, these are the people that you can trust. So in deciding whom these people are, the only question to ask is: does this person genuinely want to see me succeed or fail as I independently try to resurrect my business in the wake of the COVID-19 crisis?

# Chapter 10
# Strategy # 10: Adapt

*When you start to feel as if you have more in common with the friends who have passed away than you do with the people with whom you still live, then perhaps you have lived too long. But . . . if you feel that you would like to persevere . . . then you most certainly must learn to accept, acknowledge and adapt. Anachronisms are a curiosity and sometimes even a pleasant novelty but they are seldom an enduring success.*

It is time to be perfectly candid about it. There is no reason to beat around the bush. I have to give it to you straight so that you and your business can be properly prepared. Here it is:

The world will never be the same as what it was before!

I am sorry to have to be the one to tell you. It is a stark reality and perhaps an inescapable truth but the world as we knew it before will never be quite the same. The pandemic has been a seminal event in every person's life at this point. Its effects will long be remembered. It has changed us in many ways and the consequences of those changes will not be sorted out for some time to come.

Excuse me for being so blunt but good businesspeople prefer candor to BS. All of us who have been holding on to memories of how things were before this pandemic need to prepare mentally for what some will call the "new normal." Sadly, that is a terrible cliche and it really does not describe what the future holds. It is technically an oxymoron in that "new" implies novel, fresh, different or as of yet not previously experienced and "normal" implies a routine rooted on what one has grown accustomed to day in and day out. It will not be a "new normal" as much as what is normal in the future shall be based on a new set of circumstances and conditions which will become customary and familiar at that time. So, at this point we need to accept that the future will not consist of a "new normal" but it will simply be different.

Will we like it? Who knows?

The point is that like it or not the COVID - 19 crisis has ushered in one of those historical realities that results in change. In the wake of change, things will be different. There will be some things in the future that will be nice changes and there will be some things that will not be so nice. Some changes will seem good, some tolerable and some will just plain make us yearn for earlier times. That is the essence of change.

We have experienced changes in the past and we have adapted. When my wife and I first traveled together by plane, we arrived at the airport 20 minutes before our scheduled flight and made it to the gate and onto the plane well before it took off on time. Nowadays, in the wake of 9/11, that same process would take no less than 2-3 hours as we would go through TSA security and metal detectors, identity screening, baggage x-rays etc. At that same time land-line phones outnumbered cellular phones by an incredible margin whereas now the opposite is true. There were no smartphones then and the internet, in its infancy, was actually a useful resource for information rather than a vast wasteland of indiscriminate amounts of trivial sewage and digital social interaction predominated by narcissism.

    The point is that whether we like it or not, we have accepted change in the past. More important, we have adapted to the changes that have been imposed upon us by circumstances beyond our control. Adapting is in our DNA. It is the reason why we have evolved as we have and therefore it is one of the cornerstones of surviving. Time marches and if you do not keep adapting to different times and situations then time will walk all over you when it gets here.

    If you no longer want to accept change and adapt then no one is forcing you. You will not likely feel comfortable in the present but you are free to cling to the past. Most people adapt however and so you will find that you have fewer and fewer people with whom to relate. Nevertheless, as inevitable as change is for the vast majority of people, you are free to stay in the past. You will not thrive there and you most likely will perish eventually but you are free to remain.

If you wish to pursue a happy medium between accepting change and holding on to the past, then you are free to reminisce. There is nothing wrong in holding the past in high esteem just so long as you do not try to live in it. It is much like camping. You can harken back to a simpler time but you do not take up permanent residence in a tent. You can only crap in the woods so many times before you regret not having a toilet with functioning plumbing.

Meanwhile, if you have a business that you rely upon for your subsistence then you might want to consider accepting change and adapting accordingly. Your business has to adapt in order to stay relevant. Ten years ago you might have gotten away without a website. Today it is essential to your business. Thirty years ago you had no intention of maintaining an expensive cellular phone account. Now everyone in your business has at least one phone. The point is that your business has adapted in the past and it can do it again. Even if you personally resist change, your business cannot afford to do so. To remain relevant your business has to adapt to changes that are inevitable. Rendering your business irrelevant is that critical first step to going broke.

So, that being said, it raises a question. Does anyone know what the world will be like after the pandemic? No one can tell you for sure but there are some things that you can probably safely assume. For your purposes as a business owner, once you have accepted that fact that things will be different then you can start to implement the strategies that you will need to adapt. The two most important strategies for you will be to be flexible and be prepared to improvise.

Be flexible in how you go about things

while they are changing. Do not cut ties with your employees thinking that you will never have them back but do not hire all of them back right away if it looks as though your business will need time to get back on its feet.

Improvisation requires creativity. If you are not creative then make sure that you seek counsel and advice from people who are. As a businessperson you have developed the skills to handle things that had been problems that were "new" when you encountered them for the first time. Once you had learned how to deal with those problems then you overcame them to the point where they really were not problems any longer. Handling those things became routine. When new problems have presented themselves then you figured out how to deal with them as well. That process undoubtedly involved improvising. There will always be new problems to solve. Life will always be adding rows to your Rubic's cube. You will work on it, you will improvise and you will solve it just in time for a new layer of problems to present themselves. The process will repeat.

There was a man who made and sold buggy whips. His were the best on the market and he sold lots of them. He kept a healthy supply of the finest leather available so as to always be able to meet demand. Then, one day, he saw an automobile and he started to worry. He looked at all of the leather he had on hand and he realized that he was in a fix. He walked home that night and rather than just looking down he looked around. As he observed what people were doing and how they looked and how they were dressed a thought occurred to him. He asked himself, "do men really need suspenders?" As he thought some more he considered, "if suspenders go out of style then there probably will be one heck of a market for leather belts!"

Seems like a pretty smart guy.

## Chapter 11
## Strategy # 11: Be Prepared

*When I was young, I was briefly in the Boy Scouts. I only earned two merit badges during my short tenure. I got the one for "sports handicapping" as a result of my fondness for the race track. I then got the merit badge for "sexual awareness." Once I got that one, the idea of spending time in tents with a bunch of other guys no longer appealed to me as much as what I had learned in earning that particular merit badge.*

The Boy Scouts' motto "be prepared" can be applied as a strategy in recovering from the financial effects of COVID-19. Prior to the "pandemic" you might have had an excuse as to why your business was not prepared this time around. But, now that we know what to expect more or less, then it is fair to say that we should go about preparing never to get caught off guard to this extent ever again. Moreover, now that we have experienced this type of event, we need to take steps to be ready with a predetermined plan of action should it, or something similar, ever reoccur.

Perhaps the first thing to do is to think about stashing some cash. Although we may have stimulus checks, once we can start earning again then we need to develop a strategy for saving for that future rainy day. This is likely to be pretty hard to do as many of us get back on our feet but still we should commit to it. Face it, one of the things that would have helped this time around would have been a nest egg that could have been hatched to tide you over during the shelter in place orders. Saving is never easy but like anything else it becomes easier as it develops momentum. If you skip lunch one day then throw ten bucks in a jar. The ball games and concerts that you missed during the pandemic should provide some cash that you can toss in the drawer. Take ten percent of your salary each week and throw it into that account that you never seem to bother reconciling. Throw your spare change into a bucket and then forget about it. Slowly, before you know it, you will have a nest egg.

Meanwhile, the fact that the government closed your business so suddenly and without warning only added to the anxiety of the pandemic. Even as we assembled and stocked up on masks and gloves, being closed out of one's business unexpectedly exacerbated your problems.

Then, when they indicated that there would be an indefinite duration to the sudden cessation of your operation things only went from bad to worse. Of course, no business can be prepared for an event that will suspend it indefinitely but being prepared for temporary interruption certainly is possible. Insurance companies provide coverage for such eventualities and therefore it must be something that can be anticipated and subject to responsive planning.

Perhaps before the pandemic you could not imagine what it would be like to have your business closed. Well, now you can imagine that because you have experienced it firsthand. Now that you know what to expect you can view it in more concrete terms. The concept of having your business arbitrarily closed is no longer an abstraction. You know what it is like now and you know what issues you will need to address. You can picture how to deal with that for a day, a week, a month etc. So although you cannot plan for an indefinite shut down, you can at least figure out how to handle a shut down in small doses.

One thing we also need to do is to find effective means of government checks and balances to avoid the power to pull the plug on our economies falling into the hands of a single individual. The various governors exhibited considerably more authority than might have been appropriate under the circumstances. This level of authority in just one individual needs to be reviewed. Otherwise, we are at the mercy of governors who might not be adequately informed as to the best decisions to be made. If ever there was a time when debate should have been entertained on an issue as vital as the shutdown and virus response it was now. Some of the decisions by the various governors who employed a one size fits all attitude toward their respective states should have been subject to review by the oversight of the respective legislatures. Some governors lacked the proper capacity to fully appreciate the consequences of their actions. Some simply could not empathize with the plight of small businesses who were suddenly thrown out of business as a result of the governors' decisions. There is a little difference in the ability to be incisive or arbitrary but there is a huge difference in the consequences of being either.

The point is that we need a better response by our respective government leaders in times of crisis such as this. We need to examine the limits of executive authority and we need to implement emergency legislative procedures to review executive decisions promptly. This comes not from our businesses but from promoting active citizens and groups to lobby for changes in these instances. We need to support the people who will look into this for us. Send them money and follow them on social media. Encourage them as best you can so that they do what they can to assure that unbridled government restriction is always and forever restrained. COVID-19 has extracted a heavy toll on humans and it would be all the more tragic if it exacted a permanent toll on our liberty.

  Also, in being prepared, we need to think of ways of otherwise being capable of implementing reasonable steps to protect the public who interacts with our business. Some of these practices may be permanent and continuous. Others will be implemented exclusively when we are in pandemic mode. For example, the plexiglass barriers going up so quickly are impressive. This would seem to be fairly effective in preventing the spread of the disease. It would seem worth the investment. You can always take them down and store them should we ever experience this or some other viral infection again.

Finally, we have to be better prepared next time by finding ways of obtaining and disseminating accurate information. We cannot proceed in the future with conjecture when facts are available. We knew little about COVID-19 before it arrived but once it got here then we needed to obtain facts about it more quickly. We need to be able to find ways to dispel rumors promptly and to get information out without spin. We need to find a way to assure objectivity. Sadly, we used to have a free and objective press to help in these instances. We do not have that now and so we must find information elsewhere. The internet is not necessarily helpful as it is made up of too much information that needs to be verified and then synthesized before it can be relied on for consumption. In order to prepare, we need to get a proper handle in obtaining accurate information. We need to start vetting our sources and finding ways of castigating those who have perverted journalism as we had known it.

Lastly, we need to develop auxiliary

systems for maintaining our businesses and utilizing labor should we ever face a similar crisis in the future. People have adapted slowly to working from home but they now seem to be getting better at it. This is just one strategy to avoid the spread of the virus. We need to continue developing "touchless" interaction with customers. Avoid contact and avoid contamination. We have made great strides in this regard.

And, finally, find ways to incorporate flexibility into your business to cope with future potential shutdowns. Try to find ways to render your business a "necessary" or "essential" business that can be maintained during a future pandemic. Spend some time considering how you might go about manufacturing masks or sanitizer in order to maintain business while under a government imposed lock-down. It would be easiest to engage in some related or ancillary business or to make something similar to the type of manufacturing your company currently does but why not be more flexible? If you can find a way to create something that would be necessary in a similar crisis then you just might be able to prepare your business to remain open in the wake of future potential shutdowns.

What if you cannot manufacture something necessary in the wake of a pandemic? Then take a look at your delivery trucks. See if you can retrofit them to deliver groceries or food or other vital supplies.

The point is that being prepared is merely a matter of being creative. Now that you no longer have to be preoccupied with wondering what a shutdown in the wake of a pandemic will be like, you can focus on having your business prepared in the future. You can use your imagination to create new ways of dealing with the crisis. Creativity is often the key to preparedness. Do not take it for granted.

## Chapter 12
## Strategy # 12: Don't Judge

*The internet is a library where virtually everyone has a card and none of the books are properly organized and arranged. It seems that the fiction is mixed with the nonfiction to the point where no one knows what is real anymore. So, when someone supports an argument by introducing "facts" that they obtained from the internet . . . . well . . . .*

Remember what I said in Chapter 1 about perspective? Specifically, I pointed out that people cannot agree on how serious the crisis has been. I said that there are some people hunkered down in their hermitically sealed basements with N² 9500 masks worrying themselves to death while others are out and about as if there is no threat at all. When I referenced these very different types of people, I was trying to point out that there are varying degrees of concern about the crisis. So, naturally you may expect that different people will deal with it very differently. Some will be overly cautious while some will not care in the least. Some will heed the government's authority and some will question and potentially protest each restriction to the highest degree. Some will be satisfied to stay in place and avoid interaction at all costs while others will seek every opportunity to defy the virus and the response to it.

Meanwhile, some people will not know what to do. These individuals will fall somewhere in the middle of the spectrum. They may think that the masks look silly and to some degree the reaction to the pandemic is overly dramatic but they will try to *seem* compliant. Others will not only allow the restrictions imposed by the government as a result of the pandemic to compel their undying obedience but they will be enforcers of the restraints on our liberties to others. Some will think that these folks are overreacting while those folks will think the ones questioning it are fools. The varying degrees to which different people will take the crisis seriously or not is vast.

Moreover, just as the virus physically affects every individual differently, opinions about it and society's reaction to it vary just as differently from person to person. The degree to which people react to the pandemic does not necessarily follow throughout typical demographics. Some elderly people are fearful of it while other seniors feel they have survived far worse threats. Some young people may seemingly act irresponsibly in failing to observe social distancing while others would not allow you to pry the masks off of their faces. There will be varied reactions and opinions concerning the virus within people generally associated with different backgrounds, political leanings, ethnicity, social class etc. It seems that the reaction to the pandemic is as varied as there are different individuals across the earth. It truly is analogous to how it affects people physically.

Perhaps the problem for people in this instance is that there truly is too much information available and regrettably, not all of that information is valid. In Chapter 1 we spoke about how little we know for certain when it comes to the virus. In the absence of actual facts, we are left with theories, general opinions and assumptions. Different people will assess and process that information differently. Much of it will be subject to their own experience and viewpoint. Some will get their information from cable news outlets that unfortunately have various agendas to push and may not necessarily be *newsworthy*. Some will get their information from the internet or social media or some other source that might not be credible.

Meanwhile, some people will merely look for information to support what they want to believe about the crisis and find authority to justify their opinions and reactions. They may disregard authority that runs contrary to what they believe or they may consider it. Who can tell why or what anyone will think or do in the wake of the pandemic? To a great degree, it is not anybody's fault why each of us will think about and react to the virus as each of us individually will.

The point for your business is that regardless of how people feel about the crisis, no one should be judged regarding their feelings about it. There is nothing good that can come from thinking that the guy who is bathing in hand sanitizer every night is a "Worrisome Wilbur." Likewise, there is nothing to be gained by referring to the guy who seems oblivious to wearing a mask and social distancing a "Reckless Ralph." For all anyone *knows for sure* Wilbur might be right or Ralph might be right. Perhaps "Middle of the road Marvin" has the best perspective about it. What you will see as you attempt to run your business is that you do not need to judge any of them because in the face of the crisis, you are likely to run into all three of them at one time or another.

Being in tune with how people react to the crisis is going to be critical for your business. You may have your own opinions but those are no more important *or valid* than those of anyone else. We have already said that some are most likely overreacting while others are not taking it seriously enough. As for you, your personal opinions do not matter.

If someone is obsessed with the pandemic do not try to persuade them to be any less so. There is nothing to be gained by challenging them or even demonstrating that you differ from them. You do not have to ostensibly agree with them but there is nothing to be gained by alienating them either. Let them obsess so long as it does not affect you or lead to the potential harm of others.

Also, if someone does not take the threat the least bit seriously and refuses to observe social distancing etc. then you do not need to police them. You might want to discreetly suggest that observing the restrictions in and of themselves are not necessarily offensive. You could say that to the point that they are not overly burdensome, "what does it hurt?" You could imply that observing some level of concern is the responsible thing to do to those who are likely being oversensitive to the crisis. However, do not tell these folks that they have no right to the opinion that the whole thing is "nuts." If that is what they believe then so be it. They do not need for you or anyone else to be the opinion police.

Here is the part where my advice gets tricky particularly in the context of our current culture. For your purposes as you go about managing your business through this crisis, keep your opinion to yourself! In the time of social media where every thought is assessed to be so worthy of expression as to render it important simply because it exists and can be transmuted to one's thumbs and typed into one's phone for mass distribution, we need to learn that expressing our opinions are not all that important. Having opinions is important but expressing them in unvarnished fashion is not necessarily essential to our daily lives.

There are forums where opinions can and should be expressed. Like anything else, there is a time and place for expressing one's ideas. That time and place is not in your business however.

Your business needs to keeps its (and your) opinions to itself. Your business does not need to reflect what you think about the crisis. Just as we suggested in Chapter 7 about being apolitical, your business can be open-minded when it comes to the pandemic and the reaction to it. If a client or customer feels the need to dogmatize you with their opinion on the crisis then listen politely. Maybe you will learn something or maybe you will not. Maybe you will agree and maybe you will not. In the end, who cares? Do not let it affect your relationship with them. Do not even let it change your opinion about them. If you can sell to them regardless of their opinion then you have learned the most important lesson of all. It is a new adage indeed but here it is:

> The customer is not always right but is permitted to think that you think that he or she is.

Look, for your purposes, who cares how a customer feels about the crisis? If their money is as good as anyone else's then why should their opinion matter to you. Do not look down on someone who feels differently about the crisis than you do. Do not act like the pandemic police and embarrass someone for not wearing a mask. If it is the law where you are then tell them discreetly if possible that no one has a choice but to obey the law.

The point is that for your perspective, do not judge others. If you think about the opinions of others then it is easy to get caught up in the politics of this mess. You do not need the distraction.

Do no discriminate based on how seriously anyone treats the COVID crisis. Present an open-mindedness that makes your customers feel welcome. If they like you then they will likely just assume that you agree with them whether you do or do not. Is your opinion more important than having a customer who likes you and your business? Probably not so let them think about you what they wish.

Meanwhile, for you personally, do not take out resentment for what the crisis has done to your business on anyone else. There have been plenty of bad decisions by numerous substantially inept leaders and scientists. All we can do is hope that they meant well. If it turns out that they were acting out of malevolence of any kind then all bets are off but until that has been determined, let us hope for better.

Otherwise, keep an even keel for yourself and your business. Do not add to the acrimony of offering a difference of opinion about something about which no one has an unqualified correct opinion.

Frankly, a little less judging of one another may well be very important in our society right now. We have been making assumptions about one another that have proven wrong. We have formed opinions about one another that in many cases are undoubtedly wrong. It is time to get over ourselves and look at things from a purely business perspective. In business one harbors no bias. There is no point to maintaining prejudice or discriminating. It is best to transact business with one another with no preconceived notions and without predispositions. A good businessperson welcomes the opportunity to do business with just about anyone. You can make just as much money from someone you do not like as with someone that you do. So why not sell to both? Look for nearly every opportunity to interact with others for the sake of your business and you cannot go wrong.

## Conclusion

There is a natural tendency to be afraid when you are not in control. Think of a roller coaster. It seems like you are being thrown around defying gravity at every turn, flip and spin, unable to prevent the ride from going faster and scaring the heck out of you. 2020 Is an election year that was going to seem like a roller coaster anyway and now into the second turn the roller coaster stopped in the middle of a loop leaving us hanging upside down and wondering if any of us will survive or when and if the ride will ever resume. If that is not frightening then it is hard to say what is.

Against this metaphorical backdrop is the trauma suffered by an army of small capitalists just hoping and praying that there will be enough of their business left when this is over so as to continue to exist. It is not hard to imagine the anxiety that these poor folks must be feeling as they wonder what the post COVID-19 world will be like and whether the damage it has inflicted on their businesses can be overcome.

In writing this book I was hoping to be able to share some insight as to some of what small business entrepreneurs might be thinking. Because businesspeople do not think in terms of problems but rather they focus on solutions, I introduced the twelve strategies I have presented herein. As I said at the outset, there are many more strategies that you can learn from businesspeople much smarter than me. Even if they do not charge for the advice, buy them a drink and show your gratitude.

When I started this book, I told you to exhale. I suggested that you needed to breathe. Along the way as we went through my twelve strategies, I found a subtle way to tell you to laugh as well. Some will condemn me for even suggesting that we laugh at the seriousness of these times but I would beg to differ with those folks. Perhaps more than anything else at this juncture, we need to laugh if for no other reason than to acknowledge the absurdity of our feeble, frail and often funny responses to the obstacles that life presents for us. There are times when jokes are inappropriate but I would submit that this crisis has gone on long enough to indulge us with a little humor. Humor can often provide perspective and in this instance, we need plenty of perspective.

Moreover, a little humor here and there will not undermine the seriousness of the crisis. People understand the crisis much better than they understand the virus that is causing the crisis. It has been taken seriously since before it hit our shores. It is a potentially deadly disease. It has been respected as such. So far it has shown that a small percentage of those afflicted will die and that is tragic. Nevertheless, a vast percentage of the public will be affected in other ways and, even if that does not result in their deaths, it is no less worthy of being a tragedy.

You see, despite those who are obsessed with COVID-19, the rest of us in general are not required to be preoccupied with COVID - 19. Thankfully, it seems to be proving not to be the end all and be all of human existence and so there is nothing wrong in the consideration of other things. Given the overwhelming discipline and personal sacrifice exhibited by virtually everyone around the world who are taking steps to protect others and themselves in the wake of the pandemic, it appears obvious that people are demonstrating sufficient solidarity with the people most directly affected by the disease.

Many have abandoned their livelihoods and liberty for the sake of preventing the spread of COVID - 19. People are wearing masks, social distancing and taking other significant precautions all for the sake shielding the most vulnerable from and preventing the spread of the disease. We have done all of this based on evidence derived from debatable statistical models and somewhat inconsistent scientific opinions that have yet to demonstrate a level of accuracy that has justified our sacrifice. We have heeded the scientists out of an abundance of caution despite their inability to reach a consensus among themselves as to what we are actually accomplishing.

So, in light of this level of personal sacrifice, it is wrong when some attempt to shame people into prefacing every conversation with an acknowledgment that the disease is killing people and that everyone should be thinking about those people most affected by the disease. Everything that we are doing demonstrates that we are thinking of them. Yet, we are not required to think exclusively of them. Moreover, we are not required to forsake any reasonable skepticism over whether our government enforced compulsory reaction to the disease is justified.

Our allegiance to the preservation of life should not be used as a basis to completely surrender our liberty to local governments taking often times tyrannical steps in the name of COVID -19. Private sector individuals and businesses are being compelled to make great sacrifices by sanctimonious government officials who are collecting their salaries while proclaiming that "we are all in this together." It seems that the Pharaoh gives us no straw and yet expects no decrease in the number of bricks that we produce.

Against this backdrop, we are inundated

with message after message about what is expected of us in light of the pandemic. The general prescription that we need to stay safe and continue to take precautions and show gratitude to people working to stock the shelves and to healthcare personnel in virtually every commercial on television is becoming a little patronizing. One can give credit to advertisers who have been quick to show the human side of every client in commercial after commercial acknowledging these difficult times. The problem is that by so many companies making statements about how socially conscious they are, the act itself seems so obligatory as to ring hollow.

It is a testament to the advertising community that they have been able to adapt so quickly but over-saturation of the point leads to skepticism and in some cases contempt for clients who feel the need to promote how truly caring they are. It is certainly okay for companies to spend their advertising dollars on thanking healthcare workers. And, it makes sense that they would want to promote that they are taking steps to protect the health and safety of their customers. However, when a major company run by executives and board members who are likely flush with cash and financially well equipped to survive the pandemic, tells us that "we are all in this together" then that seems a little out of touch. I have nothing against rich executives but their expressions of solidarity in these instances seems like one camel that you cannot shove through the eye of a needle.

The truth is that pablum from advertisers telling us to hang in there is becoming somewhat tedious if not outright condescending. We can acknowledge the suffering of others while appreciating our own good fortune in not contracting the disease. We can also lament that our personal freedom has been constrained and that we are making sacrifices. We can do all of these at the same time. It does not make one a bad person for acknowledging how the pandemic affects one personally even if it does not cause one to experience physical suffering. So long as one does not lose perspective in caring for and about those who are more detrimentally affected then it is okay to feel ever so sorry for oneself. It should not be the focus of one's feelings nor should it predominate one's depth of concern but it is nothing to feel guilty about so long as one maintains perspective.

So, whether it is from a power hungry government official or an overenthusiastic advertiser, all of this pandering in the wake of the pandemic is unnecessary. People do not need to be reminded to be gracious and concerned about those suffering and about what is expected of them in light of the pandemic. We should assume that most people are fundamentally good and so they do not relish seeing others suffer or die. That premise should seem universal. If we can accept that premise then we may likely be able to put this terrible tragedy into perspective as we try to undo much of the chaos it has caused for us in going about our lives.

If we can assume that everyone feels bad about people who are sick and dying from COVID - 19 without requiring people to confirm those feelings first, then perhaps we can begin to entertain the ideas of people who are attempting to restore some semblance of normalcy as we endeavor to get past it.

You see, shameful as some would have you believe this fact to be, the goal is not merely to save lives. That is of paramount importance of course but it is not the only goal. The goal for the world is to get past the pandemic and to rectify some of the disastrous things that it has done to all of us.

Whether getting beyond the disease comes from developing a cure or some form of inoculation or vaccination, putting it behind us is critically important. Restoring our lives to what they had been prior to the disease is one of our goals. It is a worthy goal. There should not be any guilt in craving that goal and certainly no inhibitions in attempting to responsibly pursue that goal.

You see, when it comes right down to it, there is nothing wrong in longing for attending sports events, or concerts, or going to work, or going to the park, or hugging our elderly family members, or going to a party or a restaurant, or shaking hands with a friend or longing for doing any of the myriad of things that we took for granted before the pandemic. It is that longing that will motivate us to fight this virus and potentially eradicate it. It is that longing that needs to be nurtured so as to put our full attention, determination and ingenuity into solving the COVID - 19 crisis.

In some ways, the COVID - 19 crisis may be responsible for making many of us think about how much we took our lives for granted before this. If anything good can be said to have come of this then that might be something.

Meanwhile, the heartache that everyone feels over what the disease is doing to people is a compelling reason to fight it. Yet, a desire to restore those things that we all enjoyed before and yearn to enjoy again may prove similarly compelling in making the coronavirus pandemic something that we can, and will, get past.

The same hearts and the same humanity in those who have taken steps to be cautious and save others are shared by that army of capitalists who drive our economy. These are the entrepreneurs whose sacrifice should be more respected than it has been so far. Their hopefulness, and attitude, and ingenuity, and dedication, and commitment, and professionalism, and fairness and the myriad of other characteristics that motivate them to operate their businesses as they do can be reflected in all of us. These traits inspire survival and they help us to overcome challenges that only seem daunting. Dare I say it that the American spirit is rooted in entrepreneurism and that is what is likely to get all of us through this crisis.

GOOD LUCK, GOD BLESS and BE WELL!

## ACKNOWLEDGMENTS

I have so many people to thank that I am as always fearful to forget any of them. I would beg forgiveness of any who might not be acknowledged but for any weakness of my memory. Your contribution is as meaningful as any others that immediately come to mind and I assure you that you are in my nightly prayers.

That being said, I have to thank Susan, Jason and Nate. I often tell others that I am more blessed than I deserve to have them as part of my life. Should anything I ever write (or do or say) be offensive to others than I would simply ask that my family be spared any criticism or malice that anyone would direct toward me. My family has suffered enough to have to put up with me in their lives and so they would not deserve to be subjected to any malice which should rightly be directed at me.

I also wish to thank my in-laws. My late

father-in-law was an entrepreneur who taught me a lot and treated me like his own son. His kindness to me has only been surpassed by my mother-in-law who could not be more caring, loving, patient and kind to me, my wife and our sons.

When my practice needed someone to handle its administration, my father-in-law introduced me to a woman who has been more like the sister I have never had. Thanks Linda for all that you do. On its best days our office is a reflection of everything you do for it.

I am the third of four brothers each of whom are entrepreneurs in their own right. Along with their spouses, significant others and my four nephews and their wives, they have taught me so much more than I have ever fully acknowledged. I cannot tell all of them enough how much I appreciate them. Sometimes it may seem awkward to tell other adult family members that you love them but I always hope that they know that I do.

My father was the greatest businessman I ever had the good fortune to know. Along with my mother who stood by him and has always been an inspiration to my brothers and me, I could not imagine better parents. Their undying love and sacrifice for us boys will be an indelible mark on generations of Annes' to come and my gratitude to them is boundless.

    I have many other extended family members on Mom's and Dad's respective sides of the family, some of whom are still with us and some who have passed on. They too have taught me so much especially about how wonderful extended family members can be. You are all fondly thought of often and I am quite diligent in reminiscing about all of the good times we have had. Thank you for that.

    I have been blessed to have so many friends, colleagues and associates over the years. I would not deign to list them all for fear of running out of paper. So many people have been so good to me over the years and I am so blessed to have known them all. I will make a point of thanking each of you personally when we grab that drink that I seem to promise to just about all of them.

I was extremely fortunate to have my dear friend Tiny and his sister Jodie in my life before each passed at a very young age. They inspire me to be a better person as I am sure that they are in Heaven and, if all hope for me is not totally lost, perhaps I will see them again.

Finally, I have no publicist, agent, promoter, editor, proofreader, illustrator, cover designer or any of the number of other people who would otherwise be part of the process to publish a book like this. This little project, as with all the others that have preceded it, is all my own. This makes it easier for those who do not like it to focus their displeasure or outright contempt on only one responsible party. It is just little old me.

In my defense, I am a man who loves small businesses and the people who own and operate them. Through these very tough times I have stayed up late to write these meanderings so as to share some of the wisdom that has been imparted upon me over the years. If I am able to help just one business to survive COVID -19 and its aftermath with this short book then that would be worth it. However, I certainly would not complain if countless thousands or even millions paid full cover price for it either. The humanitarian hopes for the former and the businessman hopes for the latter.

## THANK YOU ALL!

www.ingramcontent.com/pod-product-compliance
Lightning Source LLC
Chambersburg PA
CBHW071410210526
45465CB00001B/322